TALK RADIO

TALK RADIO

WRITTEN BY
ERIC BOGOSIAN

CREATED BY
ERIC BOGOSIAN
AND TAD SAVINAR

THEATRE COMMUNICATIONS GROUP
NEW YORK
2007

Talk Radio is published by Theatre Communications Group, Inc.,
520 Eighth Avenue, 24th Floor, New York, NY 10018-4156.

This publication is made possible in part with public funds from the New York State Council on the Arts, a State Agency.

TCG books are exclusively distributed to the book trade by Consortium Book Sales and Distribution, 1045 Westgate Drive, St. Paul, MN 55114.

Library of Congress Cataloging-in-Publication Data
Bogosian, Eric.
Talk radio / written by Eric Bogosian ; created by Eric Bogosian and Tad Savinar.
p. cm.
ISBN 978-1-55936-324-2
1. Radio talk shows—Drama. I. Savinar, Tad. II. Title.
PS3552.O46T35   2007
812'.54—dc22
2007016250

Text design and composition by Lisa Govan
Cover design by Kitty Suen
Cover photo of Liev Schreiber from the 2007 Broadway production
of *Talk Radio* is by Joan Marcus
Author photo by Susan Johann

First Edition, June 2007

This edition is dedicated
to the memory of
Joseph Papp

PREFACE

I wrote this play during a chaotic time in my life. I was newly married, finally getting attention for my work, an agent had signed me, I was even starting to make a living. Coincidentally, my life was falling apart. I was bogged down in a "lifestyle" that had served me well since my arrival in New York City ten years earlier, but which now left me with daily hangovers and a sour attitude. Something had to give, but I wasn't sure what. I was hungry for an indefinable something. Fame? Fortune? Peace of mind? "Confusion reigned."

This play emerged from these times. It began as a collaboration between Tad Savinar, a visual artist living in Portland, Oregon, and myself. In early 1985, in Portland, Tad and I staged a performance combining projections and live callers. I played Barry Champlain.

A year later, Joseph Papp asked me if there was anything I wanted to do at The Public Theater. I took the thirty pages I had of Barry and the callers and rewrote *Talk Radio* as a play, surrounding Barry with a storyline and fellow radio-station personnel. The play, *Talk Radio*, directed by Fred Zollo, arrived without much fanfare in the spring of 1987. For four months I reprised the title character, Barry Champlain, alongside a wonderful cast. In mid-summer I left the show and Larry Pine played Barry for two more months. There was some talk of taking the play to Broadway, but Broadway was not the right venue for the play back then.

Barry evolved from earlier characters I had played either in nightclubs or in my solo shows. In many ways, he is my alter ego. He is energetic and dark. He is hopefully funny. He is insecure. He is a bully. And more than anything else, he has the soul of a performer, which is to say, his audience means everything to him.

Around that same time, producer Ed Pressman bought the rights to make a film of the play. Once we got started on the film, I asked Ed to secure the rights to the Stephen Singular book, *Talked to Death*, a biography about the life and death of Alan Berg, a popular shock-jock who was murdered in cold blood in Denver in 1984. Berg was gunned down by right-wing extremists for his upfront and incendiary views. As I wrote the script for the film, I wove in aspects of Berg's life and death. Oliver Stone came aboard to direct. We continued to finesse the screenplay, then jumped into an accelerated shooting schedule. (Stone was in pre-production on *Born on the Fourth of July*.) The film was released in late 1988, about eighteen months after the play first opened in New York.

When Oliver and I worked on the film adaptation, we had to transpose the rhythm of the play, which allowed for long, leisurely dialogue with the callers, into the rhythm of a movie, which needed a more insistent plot. With Oliver's film it became even more important that each call build the dramatic tension of the story. Plays can enjoy taking time with charismatic moments—movies cannot. Movies are like sharks—when they stop moving they die. And so some callers were deleted, others were added. Action, flashbacks, other locales were added to the story. Every line was polished.

But the skeleton of the story remained intact, the story of a man who has invented himself by entertaining his audience. A man who knows his worth by the size of his ratings. And this is a man who must finally face what he is, whether he likes it or not. Although we added a violent ending to the film, this story is the same story I presented at The Public Theater's Martinson Hall in the summer of 1987, before Oliver Stone and before Alan Berg. (The violent ending seemed right for our movie. It gave the film a cinematic as well as thematic closure.)

In 2006, nearly twenty years later, the producer Jeffrey Richards thought bringing the play to Broadway might make sense. In the last few years, an abundance of dramatic plays have been giving new life to Broadway, and Broadway now has a younger and broader audience. It felt like the right time to bring *Talk Radio* to this new audience. I looked at the polishing that had been done with the film. Director Robert Falls and I looked at the more dynamic plotting of the film. Although the play is the same play as that play presented twenty years ago, I used what I learned from the first version and the film to groom and adrenalinize the play. It looks the same, but it's different—that's the play you find here.

It's also important to note that putting the play up again required a very specific talent. It is after all a play with a very dominant central character. The role of Barry Champlain is technically very difficult, and the actor must have total command of both comic *and* dramatic chops. Finally, there has to be some sense that this guy has the vocal equipment and charisma to be a talk-radio host. The audience must feel as if they would listen to this show on their radio in their home.

I suggested one actor. And that actor, Liev Schreiber, agreed to do the role. Liev has been very generous in rethinking the play.

In sum, this play has had an unusual history, one that has brought many different creative people together in many different venues. Perhaps this is because *Talk Radio* is not really a "play" in the traditional sense of the word: it operates on various levels with the audience, it employs unseen actors while the lead is seated for most of the action, it moves forward via collage as much as by plot, it uses complex technology to create the radio station and the callers. The structure and texture were created during a long gestation process of trial and error.

During the various lives of *Talk Radio*, others have contributed to the dialogue between Barry and his callers: Tad Savinar, Fred Zollo, Oliver Stone and now Liev Schrieber and Robert Falls. I thank them all for bringing the WTLK studio to life.

EB
Spring 2007

TALK
RADIO

Production History

The original version of *Talk Radio* was produced in 1985 at the Portland Center for the Visual Arts through a grant from the National Endowment for the Arts and the Metropolitan Arts Commission.

The original New York City production of *Talk Radio* was first performed at The Public Theater/New York Shakespeare Festival (Joseph Papp, Producer), on May 12, 1987. It was directed by Frederick Zollo. It was performed by Linda Atkinson, Eric Bogosian, William DeAcutis, Susan Gabriel, Zach Grenier, Michele M. Mariana, John C. McGinley, Mark Metcalf, Peter Onorati, Robyn Peterson and Michael Wincott.

On March 11, 2007, *Talk Radio* was produced on Broadway at the Longacre Theatre. It was produced by Jeffrey Richards, Jerry Frankel, Jam Theatricals, Francis Finlay, Ronald Frankel, James Fuld, Jr., Steve Green, Judith Hansen, Patty Ann Lacerte, James Riley, Mary LuRoffe, Mort Swinsky, Sheldon Stein, Terri Childs, Timothy Childs, Style-Four Productions, Irving Welzer and Herb Blodgett, and presented in association with the Atlantic Theater Company. It was directed by Robert Falls; scenic design was by Mark Wendland, lighting design was by Christopher Akerlind, sound design was by Richard Woodbury and the costume design was by Laura Bauer; the production stage manager was Jane Grey and the stage manager was Matthew Farrell. The cast was as follows:

BARRY CHAMPLAIN	Liev Schreiber
STU NOONAN	Michael Laurence
SPIKE	Kit Williamson
LINDA MACARTHUR	Stephanie March
DAN WOODRUFF	Peter Hermann
SID GREENBERG, MALE CALLERS	Adam Sietz
BERNIE, MALE CALLERS	Cornell Womack
KENT	Sebastian Stan
DR. SUSAN FLEMING, FEMALE CALLERS	Barbara Rosenblat
RACHAEL, FEMALE CALLERS	Christine Pedi
VINCE FARBER, MALE CALLERS	Marc Thompson
JORDAN GRANT	Christy Pusz

Characters

BARRY CHAMPLAIN, "Night Talk" host
STU NOONAN, Barry's operator
SPIKE, Sound engineer
LINDA MACARTHUR, Assistant producer of "Night Talk"
DAN WOODRUFF, Executive producer, WTLK
SIDNEY GREENBERG, Financial talk show host
BERNIE, Sid's operator
KENT, Guest
DR. SUSAN FLEMING, Talk show host
RACHAEL, Susan's operator
CALLERS

Notes on Production

The action of the play takes place in the spring of 1987 on one set: the radio broadcast studios of WTLK Cleveland, where Barry Champlain's "Night Talk" is aired. Barry's console is arranged so that he sits facing the audience. The control booths, ancillary rooms, etc., sit behind plate glass, behind Barry at his console.

The calls are phoned in live by actors from offstage. The company members who double as the callers appear in various cameos in the course of the play as radio-station personnel.

An abruptly terminated call, when either Barry or the caller hangs up, is indicated by an *(x)*.

There are three ways the dialogue is heard: first, there is Barry's amplified voice, ostensibly the voice that the radio listeners hear; then, there is the in-studio mike, an intercom the studio personnel use to communicate to each other; finally, there is the unamplified dialogue that goes on between characters when they are in Barry's part of the studio, at his console.

Exits and entrances refer to people coming and going from Barry's part of the studio. When a character leaves the stage completely, the script will read: "_____ exits the station."

ANNOUNCER *(Voice-over)*: Coming up in the next hour, right after news and weather, Cleveland's most talked about radio program: "Night Talk with Barry Champlain"! Now, back to Sidney Greenberg and "Your Taxes and You"!

(Lights up on Sidney Greenberg at the console in the studio, wearing a headset, talking into his mike. In one of the control booths, behind plate glass, is his operator-sidekick, Bernie, who from his console fields the calls. The sound engineer for the radio station, Spike, also can be seen behind the plate glass. Sidney speaks rapidly and mellifluously.)

SID: . . . so we're back. Richard, you still with me?

RICHARD: Uh-huh.

SID: OK, now with the cash you have in hand from the second mortgage on the first property, the lakeview property, you've either taken a second mortgage or completely refinanced that property with an A-R-M. You have cash in hand. Whaddya gonna do with that cash?

RICHARD: Uh . . .

SID: Figuring the property's worth roughly in the neighborhood of two hundred thou, you pay off the existing mortgage of ten thou with a hundred-and-seventy-five-thousand-dollar refinancing loan. Simple arithmetic leaves you with a hundred and sixty-five thousand dollars. Now you *could* pocket that money. You could go nuts. Buy a Cadillac, go to Hawaii. But that isn't going to get you . . . *anywhere*. 'Cause you're not *using* the money. And the last thing you want to do is SELL and take the profit, because that means *capital gains tax* and *that* means you gotta send a check down to . . . yeah, you guessed it . . . our fat UNCLE down in Washington, DC . . . Don't wanna do that, so you hold on to that property! Now . . . Richard, you still with me?

RICHARD: I think so.

SID: Good. 'Cause now we're going to make you some money! Richard! Grab a paper and pencil and write all this down, because you're gonna take that hundred and sixty-five thou, fly to Florida and find yourself a mid-priced office building in the one–two million range. Use that hundred and sixty-five thou AND the fifty your Uncle Harry left you . . .

RICHARD: Henry . . .

SID: What?

RICHARD: Henry. My uncle Henry.

SID: AND the fifty your Uncle Harry left you AND you take the hundred thou you're gonna make off the second mortgage on your primary residence, put all that together and use that three hundred and fifteen thou as a DOWN PAYMENT on the office building in, let's say, New Smyrna.

RICHARD: Florida?

SID: Of course, Florida! You like oranges, don't ya? Drink a glass of juice every day, you'll never die. Now—you take the income you make on the rentals in your new office building, pay off your monthly finance payments and USE that excess income to buy either zero-coupon bonds or T-bills . . .

RICHARD: What about a Ginnie Mae?

SID: Ginnie Maes, Fanny Maes, Willy Mays, you'll be sitting pretty with a tax break in Florida, two places to go on vacation, and get this, Richard—over two million dollars worth of property! Unbelievable, but guess what Richard? Using my method, you've just become a millionaire. How 'bout that?

RICHARD: But wait, I don't understand . . .

SID (x): Alrightee, the big clock on the wall tells me it's time to wrap up this episode of "Your Taxes and You" for this evening. Stay tuned for news and weather, followed by some stimulating conversation with a man who has no peer, my esteemed colleague, Mister Barry Champlain! I'm Sidney Greenberg reminding you: "It's not how much you make, it's how much you take . . . home."

(Sidney throws off his headphones and stands. News and weather plays. Linda MacArthur, Barry's assistant producer, immediately goes to Sidney's console, cleans up and readies it for Barry.)

BERNIE: All right, we're off. You know, Sid, it's gonna be a wet track.

SID: 'Course it's gonna be a wet track, been raining all day. How they gonna keep it dry? Wipe it down with a towel?

BERNIE: Who you like in the third race?

SID: We keep talking, we're not gonna make it till the fifth. Did you see my car when you came in?

BERNIE: Your car?

SID: I'm coming out of the Pick 'n' Pay and there's this kid sittin' on the hood of my car. He's drawn circles, you know, around all the rust spots.

(They trail off into the hallway. Stu Noonan, Barry's operator, enters.)

STU: Where the hell is he?

LINDA: I don't know.

STU: You talk to him?

LINDA: Nope.

(Stu moves to his control booth. Barry enters.)

BARRY: I'm getting a *fuckin'* gun. Kill 'em all.

STU: Jesus, Barry! I was about to send out a search party.

(Barry pours himself a coffee.)

BARRY: No. Listen, I'm getting one of those Dirty Harry Magnums. Next time some fucker cuts in front of me—BOOM! That's it. Or driving ten miles an hour—BOOM! Right turn from the left lane—BOOM! There should be a competency test for drivers. If they don't pass, they get shot. On the spot.

STU: I hear you, man.

BARRY: Just leave the body in the car. A helicopter flies in with one of those giant magnets, lifts the vehicle out of the traffic, flies it out over the lake and drops it in. That's it. End of problem. So, how they hanging, Stu? Loose?

STU: Very loose.

BARRY: Lock and load. *(To Linda)* What, no hello this evening?

LINDA *(Newspaper clippings in her hand)***:** You wanna hear these?

BARRY: I'm here. Am I here?

STU: Sixty seconds to air, Bar.

(Barry gets settled at his console. Linda begins to read:)

LINDA: North-American Man-Boy Love Association has a chapter in Shaker Heights. They found a woman with sixty-seven cats in her house. She was raising them for their pelts! France reports women in underground dairies being milked for profit.

BARRY: Spike, beam me up, baby, beam me up.

LINDA: Are you listening to this?

BARRY: I'm listening, I'm listening. Yeah?

LINDA: I waited a half hour last night. In the rain.

BARRY: Something came up.

LINDA: Did it?

BARRY: Uh-huh.

LINDA: I waited. A half hour.

BARRY: See, that's you. Me? I would've left.

STU: Thirty seconds.

LINDA: Three out of four people say they prefer watching television over having sex with their spouse. A guy in San Jose, California, wants to be a surrogate mother, says he can do it. New report on AIDS . . .

BARRY: Forget AIDS. I don't want to talk about AIDS.

STU: Twenty.

LINDA: OK. Uh . . . Homeless people are living in an abandoned meat-packing plant in Willard. Some of them used to work there before it shut down . . .

BARRY: Where's Willard?

LINDA: Stu, you know where Willard is?

STU: Here we go in ten.

LINDA: By the way, if you called me you would know that Dan is trying to find you.

BARRY: Why?

LINDA: Something's on his mind. He's nervous.

BARRY: I'll make him nervous.

(Theme music.)

ANNOUNCER *(Voice-over)*: And now from the heart of the Great Lakes, it's time for Cleveland's most popular and controversial talk show—"Night Talk with Barry Champlain"! And now, ladies and gentlemen, here's Barrrrry!

BARRY: Last night an eighty-year-old grandmother was murdered on Euclid Avenue. Twenty people were watching, not one lifted a finger. Some kids needed cash for crack, so they stuck a knife in Grandma. In Shaker Heights, our good citizens (doctors, lawyers, dentists) have formed a little club—they're having sex with *children*. And on the west side, fifteen churches were busted last week for—get this—illegal gambling activities. And that's just here within the Cleveland city limits. This country, where culture means pornography and slasher films; where ethics means pay-offs, graft and insider trading; where integrity means lying, whoring and intoxication . . . this country is rotten to the core, this country is in deep trouble . . . and somebody better do something about it. 555-T-A-L-K. Open your mouth and tell me what we're gonna do about the mess this country is in. Let's go to the first caller. Francine!

FRANCINE: Yes, hello?

BARRY: You're on, Francine.

FRANCINE: Yes, oh . . . is this Barry?

BARRY: How's your life tonight?

FRANCINE: I have a little problem I'd like to discuss.

BARRY: Shoot.

FRANCINE: What?

BARRY: Shoot. Shoot. Let's hear it.

FRANCINE: I'm a transsexual.

BARRY: Yeah, I kinda figured that, Francine.

FRANCINE: Do you know what a transsexual is, Barry?

BARRY: Let me ask the questions, hon.

FRANCINE: Well, OK, I'm trying to save money for an operation.

BARRY: Francine.

FRANCINE: What?

BARRY: This is boring.

FRANCINE: No it isn't!

BARRY: You're a transsexual saving up for an operation? You're a cliché. Call Larry King in DC. I'll give you his toll-free number.

FRANCINE: Let me finish what I was saying!

BARRY: Francine, in your wildest imagination . . . what possible interest would your personal adventures in surgery hold for my listeners?

FRANCINE: I don't care about your listeners, this is something I have to talk about.

BARRY: Yes. But I don't. *(x)* "Night Talk." Yeah, Josh.

JOSH: Thanks a lot, Barry. Uh, Barry, don't you think that the policies of the World Bank only hurt economies of third-world countries to the benefit of American banks?

BARRY: Huh? "Third-world countries"? "Third-world countries"? Where'd you learn that phrase, in college? Something you saw on *Sixty Minutes*?

JOSH: It's a commonly used term.

BARRY: Sure. I hear it all the time. You happen to know what it means?

JOSH: Of course I do.

BARRY: Please enlighten us . . .

JOSH: Well, it means developing countries . . . small poor countries.

BARRY: Small countries . . . so India's not "third world."

JOSH: Well, India is—

BARRY: What about communist countries . . . Red China for instance?

JOSH: No, not communist countries . . . we're getting off the track . . . what I was trying to point out—

BARRY: We're not getting off the track, Josh, we're getting *on* the track. The track is you don't know what the hell you're talking about. You call me up and start spouting a mouthful of left-wing mumbo-jumbo thinking you've got a point to make. But you have no point because you are simply repeating spurious crap. Yugoslavia is communist, it's a third-world country, so's Nicaragua, so's Cuba. Josh, go back to college, and when you graduate, gimme a call . . . *(x)* "Night Talk," you're on . . .

RHONDA: Hello, Barry, this is Rhonda from Coventry. I just want to express my outrage.

BARRY: About what?

RHONDA: About what they just did up in Detroit. Giving out needles to drug addicts.

BARRY: They have to do it, hon, they're trying to stop AIDS. Clean needles help.

RHONDA: It's immoral for this country's tax dollars to be going to addicts.

BARRY: But it's all right, Rhonda, for our tax dollars—about four billion of them to go into a "drug war" that's a complete joke? You're right, Rhonda. More drugs than ever are coming into this country and guess who's bringing them?

RHONDA: Umm . . .

BARRY: We are, Rhonda! That's right, Uncle Sam and the good ol' C-I of A!! How do you think they pay for all those covert wars? Laos, Cambodia, Nicaragua, Air America, Iran-Contra, it's a time-honored tradition. You know what I say? Legalize the stuff! It would end the single greatest threat to democracy this country has ever known. Legalize drugs! Put the CIA and the mob out of business simultaneously!

RHONDA: Well that's just the dumbest thing I've ever heard—

BARRY: Is it? I think a junkie should be able to walk into a drugstore, sign his name, and get the stuff for a buck . . . That way he doesn't have to rob or kill somebody just to get a fix. Am I right?

RHONDA: What about the children, Barry? You can't let the children have drugs—

BARRY: Why not? They're gonna get 'em anyway. At least this way we control the dose! Drugs aren't the problem, Rhonda, *America* is.

RHONDA: Well I'm not sure what you mean by that but—

BARRY: Rhonda, let me ask you something. Who's the vice-president of this country?

RHONDA: George Bush.

BARRY: And what did he do before he was vice-president?

RHONDA: Well . . . uh—

BARRY: He ran the CIA, Rhonda!! You see what I'm getting at here?

RHONDA: Well, I have to disagree with you there, Barry. Maybe you haven't heard, but this is "Morning in America"—we need George Bush to complete what President Reagan—

BARRY: Oh yeah, that's just what we need! Another spook in the White House. What's a matter, Rhonda, Watergate wasn't enough for you? Listen, if you're so worried about drugs killing people, make tobacco illegal. It kills more people than cocaine, heroin and any other drug you can think of—combined!

RHONDA: But that's not what we're talking about. We're talking about drugs—

BARRY *(x)*: Thanks for the call, Rhonda. "Night Talk," and we have Junior on the line.

JUNIOR: Barry! Yeah, hey man, what do you think about the Indians this year?

BARRY: In a word, they suck.

JUNIOR: Hey, I disagree with you on that one, Bar! They're gonna take the pennant. Niekro's gonna win twenty!

BARRY: Are you nuts? Niekro's fifty years old!

JUNIOR: Well listen, you mister fuckin' big shot, Niekro has played better ball than any other—

BARRY *(x):* Yeah, yeah, yeah. The Indians are gonna be watching the series on the boob tube. Toronto will take the pennant and the Astros will take the series. On that deep note, let's break for a commercial . . . this is "Night Talk." *(Into in-studio mike)* Stu, let's cool it with the baseball calls and the transvestites tonight, all right?

STU: You got it, Bar.

BARRY: How are the lines?

STU: Looking good! I've got five hanging.

(Linda brings over a small stack of headshots.)

BARRY: You still mad at me?

LINDA: Yes.

(Beat.)

BARRY: How about now?

LINDA: Yes.

(Dan Woodruff, the executive producer of WTLK, enters as Barry autographs the photos.)

DAN: Barry . . .

BARRY: Hi, Dan.

DAN: Barry, you get my messages?

BARRY: Been very busy, Dan, very busy.

DAN: Barry, I've been speaking to Chuck Dietz. He's my guy up at Metroscan. We've been talking . . . almost every day. Twice a day.

BARRY: Dan . . .

DAN: Metroscan, Barry. Three hundred and fifty-seven affiliate stations.

BARRY: Metroscan, yeah. So what? What about Metroscan?

DAN: Dietz likes this show. A lot.

BARRY: And???? What, Dan, what? Spit it out!

DAN: He thinks you're really something. He thinks you're funny.

BARRY: Great. Linda, send him an autographed picture. Thanks for coming by, Dan.

DAN: Metroscan is thinking about picking up the show for national syndication.

BARRY: What?

DAN: They dropped a show, so they gotta make a decision by Monday. They'd just pick up the feed, link it nationally. Calls come in on a toll-free—

BARRY: Wait a minute.

STU: Sixty seconds, Bar.

BARRY: Wait a minute. What the fuck is going on here? Don't I get a say in this? Did you even call my agent?

DAN: Of course I called your agent, Barry. But you don't return *his* calls either. Dietz has got all the execs together, they're listening tonight.

BARRY: You knew about this?

LINDA: My mom thinks it's great.

BARRY: Your mom? You told your mom and . . .

(Linda exits.)

DAN: Testing the water. That's all. If it works, it works. Just make it good tonight and we're in. Congratulations, Barry. We did it.

BARRY: No, Dan, not "we"—apparently you did it.

STU: Thirty seconds, Bar.

DAN: I'm out, I'm out. I'll leave you guys alone. Make it a hot show tonight.

BARRY: Always a hot show, Dan.

DAN: But tonight extra hot. Don't wanna fuck this up. We're talking about a commitment for six months, we want six years.

(Dan exits Barry's studio, but lingers around a while to overhear the show.)

STU: Six seconds.

(Theme music.)

ANNOUNCER *(Voice-over)*: You're listening to "Night Talk with Barry Champlain." And now, back to Barry!

BARRY *(Into his mike)*: Metroscan Broadcasting is a multimedia corporation specializing in broadcast radio. It has three hundred and fifty-seven affiliate stations in the United States and Canada. *(Beat)* Two minutes ago I received a phone call from the president of Metroscan Broadcasting. He asked me if they could pick up this show, pick up "Night Talk" for national syndication starting Monday night. Now you're probably wondering why the corporate types down at Metroscan would want a guy like me, a big mouth, someone who isn't afraid to tell it like it is, running his mouth on all those stations. I'll tell you why. Money. Advertising dollars. Ratings. I got the ratings, kids. And the reason I've got the ratings is because of you, my listeners. *(Beat)* So if any of you out there are worried that Barry might soften his touch, ease up, change his style for a national show, let me put your mind at ease. That's impossible. Can't be done. *(Beat)* This great country of ours needs someone to wake it up, to shake it up and tell the truth for a change. And that someone is *me*. So I told the president of Metroscan Broadcasting—take it or leave it! *(Beat)* Well, folks, he took it. That means this show, "Night Talk," goes national starting Monday night. You put me here, folks, and I love you for it. Democracy is a wonderful thing. *(Beat)* So here's what I need you to do. There's a device in your home called a "telephone." I want you to pick it up . . . go ahead, take your hand out of the potato-chip bowl, reach out, grab your phone, hold it up to your face and dial 555-T-A-L-K. That's 5-5-5-T-A-L-K. We're going national, kiddies. You better have something to say, I know I do.

(Barry punches a button on his console.)

Ruth, you're on.
RUTH: You're such a good man.

(Ruth's voice echoes electronically.)

BARRY: Hello? You need to turn your radio down.
RUTH: You're so good, you care so much. What?
BARRY: You need to turn your radio down.

(Ruth's voice returns to normal.)

RUTH: OK. Yes, Ruth, this is Ruth. I was just listening to what you were saying, Barry, and you're so right! There is no more love, Barry. There is no more hope!
BARRY: That wasn't exactly what I was saying. I was saying that I can't help but wonder—
RUTH: No, no, you're right, Barry. Look at the world today. Hundreds of thousands of people starving in Africa and no one cares. That's all. They'll die. And it can't be stopped, Barry.
BARRY *(Into in-studio mike)*: Dr. Boozenstein to the O.R., please.
RUTH: Who can stop the toxic wastes, the terrorism, the nuclear buildup, the assassinations! They tried to kill the pope, Barry! What about that? They killed Jack Kennedy!
BARRY: Yeah, I think I remember reading something about that. Listen, Ruth, you can't take the world's problems personally.

(Linda enters with a bottle of bourbon and a glass. She pours Barry a stiff drink.)

RUTH: No, Barry, don't deny it. Don't act naive for our sake. You know the truth because you are an educated and wise man. And you're a courageous man to tell it. I'm so glad your show will finally be heard all over this country, because it's high time people started to listen to someone with a level head.

BARRY: Especially people like you, eh, Ruth?

RUTH: The pollution is killing the trees, animals are going extinct. No more elephants, no more eagles, no more whales, not to mention the rhinos, the condors, the grizzlies, the panda bears. No more *panda bears*! What's the point—will someone please tell me that?

BARRY: Ruth, cheer up! Somehow the world will struggle on without the panda bears: "Every cloud has a silver lining."

RUTH: That's nice of you to say, Barry. You're just saying that to make us all feel better. Because you are so good and kind. But, Barry, we don't deserve it. We don't deserve your love. We did this to ourselves. It's all our own fault.

BARRY: Look, Ruth, the truth is, I feel—

RUTH: It's all our own fault. Thank you, Barry, for being such a good man. You are a prick in the conscience of this country. If it weren't for you, I don't know what I'd do . . . Take care of yourself and good luck with your new show. We need it more than ever. *(x)*

BARRY: Ruth? I guess we lost Ruth. No more panda bears, no more Ruth. Gonna miss 'em. Hey, Stu, did she just call me a prick?

STU: She called you a prick, Bar.

BARRY: I think she called me a prick! Makes you think. What do you think? What do you say? Call me, I want to know. "Night Talk," Glenn, from Corlett. Hello, you're on.

GLENN: Hello, Barry?

BARRY: You got 'im.

GLENN: I'm a little nervous. This is my first time calling.

BARRY: I'll be gentle.

GLENN: Huh?

BARRY: What's on your mind tonight?

GLENN: Well first of all, I'm a long-time listener, first-time caller. Used to listen to you in Akron!

BARRY: Ah, the hippie days.

GLENN: Yeah, heh-heh. You were great then, too.

BARRY: Yeah, OK. Thanks a lot, Glenn. What do you want to talk about?

GLENN: Well, something that woman was saying about the whales?

BARRY: Whales?

GLENN: Well, going extinct. And I was thinking about the baby seals. Them, too.

BARRY: Uh-huh. Ecology . . . and?

GLENN: Yeah . . . well what I wanted to talk about was more about animals in general. We should respect our animals. I have a cat, Muffin, and, uh, sometimes, I will come home from work and we, well, I make dinner, we have, uh, dinner together, you know?

BARRY: You have dinner with your cat? At the table, you have dinner? What, with a tablecloth, candles, that kind of thing?

GLENN: Well, no, heh-heh, of course not . . .

BARRY: Oh.

GLENN: She has her own plate. On the floor . . .

BARRY: Oh good!

GLENN: Muffin has the sweetest face. You can tell exactly what she's thinking.

BARRY: Really? How 'bout an example?

GLENN: Well, I used to give her the canned cat food, right? But I could see from the expression on her face, she wanted to eat what I was eating. So now we eat the same things. I have pork chops, she has pork chops. I have a veal, she has a veal.

BARRY: Uh-huh.

GLENN: And anyway. We spend time together . . . and sometimes I just think that, well, there are so many crazy, loud people in the world. And then there's Muffin. Quiet, not hurting anybody, clean. Why can't people be more like that?

BARRY: Lemme ask you something, Glenn. You and Muffin sound pretty intimate there. You're not into anything funny are you? I mean, she's fixed, right?

GLENN: Huh? I don't like what you're saying about my cat?!

BARRY: There's a word for loving animals a little too much. Getting too intimate.

GLENN: It's not like that.

BARRY: OK, but I mean, Glenn, Muffin's fixed. Maybe the way to get people to act more like Muffin is to get *them* fixed. How 'bout that idea? Snip off the old cojones?

GLENN: No, that's not what I'm getting at at all! I don't think . . .

BARRY: You don't think? You don't think? Maybe we should all get fixed. Make life a whole lot easier. Then we'd all be quiet like little kittens. Is that what you want, Glenn?

GLENN: No!

BARRY: Why are we alive, Glenn? We are not house cats! Glenn, you got a choice, either start living or go get fixed. Take my advice, stop hanging around the pussy and go get some. *(x)* "Night Talk," Chet.

CHET: You think you're so smart.

BARRY: Hello?

CHET: You're so smart, aren't ya? Cutting everybody off 'cause you don't like what they're saying, what they're about. Why don't you cut me off?

BARRY: I will if you don't get to the point.

CHET: You know everything, don't ya?

BARRY: Not everything, Chet, no one can know everything. As hard as it is to believe, even *I* don't know everything.

CHET: Why are you always putting our country down? Why are you always talking about drugs and Negroes and Jews? Isn't there anything else to talk about?

BARRY: You know what I hate, Chet? I hate people who call me up and tell me what they *don't* want to talk about. If you *don't* want to talk about drugs or blacks, why bring 'em up in the first place? Huh? Sounds to me like you *like* talking about them. If you don't want to talk about 'em, tell me what you *want* to talk about—or get off the phone!

CHET: I want you to start telling the truth.

BARRY: About *what*, Chet?

CHET: The people behind your show, the people who pay your bills.

BARRY: The sponsors.

CHET: Don't act dumb with me. What kind of name is "Champlain" anyway? That's not a real name. You changed it, didn't you? Why? Maybe because it sounded a little too Jewish? Change the name, get a nose job, same old story. You think people are stupid? You think no one's as smart as you are? You think people are never gonna find out that you're nothing but a mouthpiece for your bosses and the State of Israel, propaganda that a bunch of Zionists are perpetrating on the American—

BARRY: Wait a sec, wait a sec . . . Hold on! State of Israel, State of Israel? Come on!

CHET: You know there are two kinds of Jews—

BARRY: Oh, this should be good.

CHET: The sneaky, quiet types and the big-mouthed types. And you're one of the big-mouthed types. Cut me off, I know you're gonna do it, go ahead!

BARRY: I'm not going to cut you off, Chet. You're too fascinating to cut off . . . You make me think—no, correct that, you remind me of a little story. Two years ago, I visited Germany, never been there before, thought I'd take a look at Hitler's homeland. Are you familiar with Adolf Hitler, Chet?

CHET: I know my history.

BARRY: Good . . . Now I decided to visit what is left of a concentration camp on the outskirts of Munich: Dachau. You join a little tour group, go out by bus, everyone gets out at the gates . . . It's rather chilling. A sign over the gates says: "Arbeit Macht Frei." It means "work will make you free," something the Nazis told their prisoners . . . Of course most of them never left . . . Are you still listening, Chet?

CHET: I hear all your lies—

BARRY: Good, feel free to take notes. Now as I walked along the gravel path between what remained of the barracks, where the prisoners slept, and the gas chambers, where they died, I saw something glitter in the gravel. I bent down to see what it was. What I found was a tiny Star of David. Very old. Who knows? It might have belonged to one of the prisoners of the camp, perhaps a small boy torn from his parents as they were dragged off to the slaughterhouse . . . I kept that Star of David . . . I know I shouldn't have, but I did. I keep it right here on my desk. I like to hold it sometimes. *(Swirling his glass of booze and studying it)* In fact . . . well, I'm holding it right now . . . I hold it in my hand to give me courage . . . maybe a little of the courage that that small boy had as he faced unspeakable evil can be passed on to me as I face the trials in my own life . . . when I face the cowardly and the narrow-minded . . . the bitter, bigoted people who have no guts, no spine, so they lash out at the helpless . . . The grotesquely ignorant people like you, Chet, who make me puke . . . People who have nothing better to do than to desecrate history, perhaps . . . only to repeat it . . . Are you still with me, Chet? *(Pause)* CHET!

CHET: Keep talkin', Jewboy, life is short. *(x)*

BARRY: Uh-huh. And, Stu, let's send a microwave oven out to Chet . . . "Night Talk," Debbie, you're on.

DEBBIE: Hello, Barry? Oh, I can't believe I'm actually on!

BARRY: You're actually on, Debbie. What's on your mind tonight?

DEBBIE: My boyfriend.

BARRY: How old are you, Debbie?

DEBBIE: I'm sixteen, Barry, and—

BARRY: Going to school?

DEBBIE: Yes, ummmm—

BARRY: And your boyfriend, what's he, a senior or something?

DEBBIE: He, uh, doesn't go to school, Barry—

BARRY: Doesn't go to school, where's he work?

DEBBIE: I don't see him all the time, so I don't really know . . .

BARRY: You don't know whether your boyfriend works or not? That's interesting.

DEBBIE: Well, see, the reason I don't know is that he leaves town sometimes, and he kind of lives in his pickup truck. It's one of those that's all customized, with tons of chrome on it . . . He even has license plates that say: "STAN-3" and everything and, ummmm, he tells me that he loves me, Barry, and I love him—

BARRY: Uh-huh. Love is a hard thing to define. Sixteen, huh? Tell me something, Debbie, is he a nice guy?

DEBBIE: Yes.

BARRY: Well, you're a lucky girl to have a nice guy with a pickup truck in love with you. So what's the problem?

DEBBIE: Well, see, I, um . . . *(Quiet)*

BARRY: Debbie, hello? You still with us?

DEBBIE: Yes . . . *(Sniffling)*

BARRY: Debbie?

DEBBIE *(Outburst)*: I'm going to have a baby, Barry . . . and now Stan isn't around. I'm going to have to tell my parents pretty soon . . . *(Whimpering)*

BARRY: Now, now, hold on there, Deb. It's not that bad. You're pregnant. We used to call it "being in trouble." It's bad, but it's not the worst thing that could happen.

DEBBIE: But my parents are gonna kill me, you don't understand!

BARRY: Look at it this way, people have babies all the time. It's not the end of the world, it's the beginning! A little baby is coming! A little pink baby! Things could be worse, a lot worse. You could be sick, or dying. Stan could be driving around in his pickup truck and have a head-on collision, go through the windshield and die!

DEBBIE: I want to die.

BARRY: No you don't, young lady.

DEBBIE: Yes I do!

BARRY: No you don't! Now let's not start taking ourselves too seriously here . . . You got yourself in a little trouble. You let your animal passions get out of hand and now the fiddler has to be paid, Debbie, right?

DEBBIE: But, Barry . . . he told me that—

BARRY: Right? Am I right or am I wrong? You liked the feel of sex, you liked the feel of being in love, you better like the feel of being pregnant.

(Debbie cries.)

Hey, now, no crying. Crying isn't going to fix anything. You're just gonna get the baby all upset. Debbie. Debbie. Now listen to me . . . is the baby kicking?

DEBBIE: No, of course not, I just found out! *(Crying)*

BARRY: What?

DEBBIE: I just barely found out!

BARRY *(Laughing)*: Well, gee, the way you're going on there, you sound like you're in labor! Come on! Snap out of it . . . Debbie, can I ask you a serious question?

DEBBIE: What?

BARRY: Do you understand what has happened?

DEBBIE: I wish I wasn't pregnant and I could go to school!

BARRY: Yes, but, Debbie, are you sorry for what you've done?

DEBBIE: Huh?

BARRY: Are you genuinely sorry for what you did to Stan?

DEBBIE: Stan? But Stan did it to me!

BARRY: No, no, no. Debbie . . . You're not listening to me . . . Now listen to me, Debbie!

DEBBIE: What?

BARRY: It takes two to tango! You seduced poor old Stan with your cute little sixteen-year-old body, and now you want everybody to feel sorry for you! You did it so you could trap Stan into sticking around. Right? No wonder the guy can't find a job! Right?

DEBBIE: Uh . . .

BARRY: That's what I think happened. You think maybe that's what happened?

DEBBIE: I don't know . . . I guess so.

BARRY: Well then you have to deal with the consequences, hon.

DEBBIE: Uh . . . but . . .

BARRY: OK, Debbie, listen. This is what we're gonna do. We're gonna find Stan. Someone out there knows where he is, and I want them to call me here at the station . . . You leave your number with Stu and we're gonna call you as soon as we come up with something. And we will, don't worry. And let me say to anybody listening right now who knows where Stan is, you know, the guy who lives in the pickup truck, the one with all the chrome and the vanity plates that say: "STAN-3." Remember folks, not one, not two, but: "STAN-3." Don't call the police . . . give me a call at 555-T-A-L-K, because we got a little girl here who's lookin' for her daddy . . . OK, Debbie?

DEBBIE: Uh . . . yeah . . . I guess . . .

BARRY: You're not gonna do anything crazy?

DEBBIE: No.

BARRY: Good. Stay warm, drink lots of milk, and stay away from the stuff under the sink and we'll talk in a little while . . . *(x)* Family radio. For the whole family. Even the unborn. We've got a pretty free-wheeling show for you tonight. You call it, we'll talk about it. Your state of mind, the state of the union, whatever statements you wanna make, we're listenin'. Hello, Cathleen.

CATHLEEN: Yes, am I on?

BARRY: You're on.

CATHLEEN: Boy, oh boy, lots of good stuff to talk about tonight.

BARRY: What's up, Cathleen?

CATHLEEN: I loved what you were saying about your show going national and everything. It's important to say all that stuff . . .

BARRY: Someone's gotta do it, hon.

CATHLEEN: I know, I know. I don't miss one of your shows, because you tell it like it is, Barry. God bless ya! God bless ya! My best friend, Judy, she hates the show and she doesn't understand why I listen . . . but to each his own, that's what I say. You tell it like it is and you've got guts . . .

BARRY: I'm glad you feel that way . . .

CATHLEEN: Judy thinks your show is for nutjobs and psychos. But I don't agree. You say a lot of good stuff.

BARRY: Yeah, Cathleen, I think you have to be more careful how you choose your friends.

CATHLEEN: Yeah, I don't like her that much anyway.

BARRY: She doesn't sound very likable.

CATHLEEN: Only problem is she's my only real friend, Barry.

BARRY: Oh yeah? I don't think someone who calls your beliefs "nutty" and "psycho" is a very good friend. You got a real friend here, Cathleen.

CATHLEEN: You're kidding me.

BARRY: I don't kid when I'm talking about something serious like friendships. As your friend, I'm giving you good advice when I tell you to stay away from Judy. She's a bitter, cynical, pessimistic person.

CATHLEEN: Maybe you're right.

BARRY: Of course I'm right. Thanks for the call. *(x)* And we have Kent on the line. Hello, Kent.

KENT: Uh, I need help.

BARRY: Shoot.

KENT: What?

BARRY: Shoot. Shoot. Tell me what the problem is.

KENT: Well I party a lot you know, with my girlfriend.

BARRY: How old are you, Kent?

KENT: Eighteen.

BARRY: How old is your girlfriend?

KENT: She's seventeen.

BARRY: All right, go ahead.

KENT: So, we, uh . . . like to, uh . . . party, you know.

BARRY: Kent. When you do all this partying, where are your parents?

KENT: They go away a lot. Vacations.

BARRY: Where are they right now?

KENT: I don't know.

BARRY: You don't know.

KENT: They're on a vacation . . . Wait a minute, I remember . . . uh . . . Fiji. Is that right? Is there a place called Fiji?

BARRY: Your parents are on vacation in a place called "Fiji." And you and your girlfriend are "partying."

KENT: Yeah . . . except . . . well, that's what I wanted to ask you about. Uh, we've been partying for a couple of days.

BARRY: A couple of days? Wait a minute, what do you mean exactly when you say "partying"?

KENT: You know, having sex . . . getting high . . .

BARRY: "Getting high"? Smokin' pot?

KENT: Well, yeah, we always smoke, but, uh . . .

BARRY: If you always smoke whaddya mean by "getting high"?

KENT: Freebase. Smokin' coke. Crack.

BARRY: Sounds pretty sordid. You've been smokin' weed and crack for a couple of days . . . with your girlfriend. What else . . . you been doing?

KENT: And drinkin'. And I dunno. I drank some Wild Turkey yesterday 'cause I was gettin' paranoid . . . Jill was doin' acid, I think. I'm not sure. Some valiums.

BARRY: You don't need to call *me*, Kent—you need to call a doctor and have your stomach pumped! Lemme give you a number . . .

KENT: Yeah, but . . . see, that's why I'm callin' you, Barry!

BARRY: Why?

KENT: Jill . . . she . . . uh, she's been sleepin' and uh . . .

BARRY: No. No. No.

KENT: She's been sleepin' and she won't, uh . . . wake up, you know?

BARRY: Don't waste my time with this crap.

KENT: Hey, she won't wake up! She's turning . . . kinda blue!

BARRY: Kinda blue . . . you just tell Stu your address and we'll send—

KENT: Hey, no, you gotta help my girlfriend.

BARRY: Tell Stu where—

KENT: No . . . that . . . I can't . . . I can't . . . *(x)*

(After Kent hangs up, dial tone.)

BARRY: Confusion reigns in Cleveland tonight. Stu, see if you can find a copy of Miles Davis' *Kind of Blue* while we break for a little commercial consolation. And in sixty seconds we'll be back with more "Night Talk." *(Switching to in-studio mike)* What's the problem tonight, Stu? You're throwing me some real curveballs.

STU: I thought you liked curveballs, Bar.

BARRY: Control, Stu, control! I don't need shit like that tonight. Something on your mind? Something wrong at home? Old lady wouldn't do the wild thing?

STU: No, Bar, Cheryl and I are doin' great . . .

BARRY: Well, then stay on the ball, all right? Gimme the meat, not the poison.

STU: You got it.

BARRY *(Making his way over to Stu):* Lemme see your board. Come on, run it! Who's this Henry guy, this nukes guy? You didn't gimme that. What about this Denise? I didn't get that either. What about the professor?

STU: Bar, the professor's a stiff. All those people are stiffs. You want stiffs, I'll shoot you stiffs.

BARRY: Stu . . . Stu . . . Stu . . . Stu . . . I don't want stiffs. Am I speaking English? Read my lips. Do your fucking job. Keep the show moving, gimme stuff I can work with! You having trouble understanding me tonight?

STU: No, Barry, I am not having trouble understanding you. In fact, I read you loud and clear.

BARRY: Good!

(Barry moves off to a control room. Stu moves forward and addresses the audience:)

STU: I met Barry Champlain in 1972. I deejayed at a "progressive rock" station down in Akron. Those were the days. Hair down to my ass. Perpetually stoned. Spinnin' nothin' but the Dead and the Allman Brothers and all that. Jethro Tull. Remember Tull? Sweet. *(Sotto voce)* "Here's one from Tull that's guaranteed to blow your mind." Right? I mean, right? Then one day, this guy shows up from Cambridge, Mass. At least that's where he said he came from. Kept his hair in a big bushy afro. And he was totally into the subversive radio thing. Much more extreme than me. We'd hang out around each other's show, throwing down tequilas and sucking limes while playing "Let It Bleed" twenty-five times in a row, just for the effect. Barry Champlain would go beyond the tolerable.

One time we did a whole show in—get this—Armenian. Another time we found this record with a kind of amazing skip in it. Just left it on. And there's this record going round and round and round and the station manager is pounding on the studio door . . . They actually had to take the door off its hinges just to stop the record. Barry didn't get fired. He got a raise.

And the more I listened to Barry, the more I wondered why I was a deejay at all. Barry would get in the saddle to do his show and one minute he's discussing Jane Fonda's nipples, and the next he's giving out the home phone numbers of every FBI agent in the state.

Then he decided to have people call in to the station. No one had ever done this in Akron before, and I tell you man, I couldn't go home! I was transfixed. Watching all this energy coming out of Barry.

And more and more people would call in to the show. The lines were jammed. 'Cause Barry would say things like: "Call me and tell me about your worst experience with a cop," and people would do it. Or he'd say: "Call me and tell me about your most spectacular orgasm," and the rest of the show would be off to the races.

Then one night, this Vietnam vet calls in. Starts rambling on about "the 'Nam." About the things he'd seen over there. The stories are lurid. Worse than any movie. Black-market weapons sales. Drug dealing by enlisted men. Guys falling in love with prostitutes. It's incredible, right? But Barry has this sixth sense. He knows there's more. Something deeper. Keeps pushing the guy.

Finally, Barry gets the vet to confess that he murdered his own commanding officer. Shot him in the back of the skull with his M-16 during a firefight outside of Khe Sahn. Killed him in cold blood. And has never told this to anybody. The guy's crying on the air. Weeping. Blubbering. Asking Barry for forgiveness. Man, it was primal. We had that vet on for almost two hours. No commercials. Just Barry and the guy.

That night was a turning point. When we finally broke for the news and weather, there was a gleam in Barry's eye. He'd seen God—in the mirror.

When he got the show in Cleveland, I said to hell with being a deejay; I jumped ship and went to work for him. I listen to Barry Champlain take off for outer space every night. Then the show's over and we go home. I mean, I go home to Cheryl and our kid . . . Barry . . . I don't know what Barry Champlain does anymore . . . It's not like the old days . . . now he just splits, says he has work to do on the show. And I can see him sitting at home making cups of coffee, chain-smoking, reading the fucking encyclopedia.

You see for Barry, talking is living. The world—his voice is what's holding it all together. Making it make sense. He talks and all those people out there become a part of him. Part of his soul. I do too, I guess . . . *(Returns to his console)*

(Barry reenters during the end of Stu's speech and sits at his console.)

BARRY: John, calling from Lorain.

JOHN: Barry, I'd like to comment if I may on the . . . what that man was saying a few minutes ago, the one who called you a Jew.

BARRY: Yeah?

JOHN: Nothing wrong with being Jewish.

BARRY: No?

JOHN: Of course not! First of all, I'm black.

BARRY: Good for you. You wanna medal?

JOHN: I mean I like you Jews and . . .

BARRY: I like you blacks, everyone should own one.

JOHN: Heh-heh. Now don't go playing me like them other folks. The point is, I have many friends who are Jewish.

BARRY: How many?

JOHN: Oh . . . I don't know, three or four.

BARRY: I wouldn't call that many . . .

JOHN: They're very nice people. Very educated.

BARRY: Yeah, John, what's your point?

JOHN: The point is, Jewish culture is a noble and ancient—

BARRY: I don't know how to break this to you, John, but they're never gonna let you into the B'nai B'rith.

JOHN: Heh-heh. That's not what I—

BARRY: Hey, John, you're black? . . . Don't you know how Jews feel about blacks? They hate you. Ever visit those slums on the East Side where the rats eat little black babies for breakfast? Jews *own* those slums . . . the banks, Hollywood.

JOHN: Well, that's all an exaggeration.

BARRY: Is it? You said Jews are educated? What does that make blacks? Uneducated?

JOHN: No, I didn't say that!

BARRY: But you did. You said Jews are educated, nice people: "I like Jews very much." That's what you said. What are you, some kind of Uncle Tom?

JOHN: What the hell do you know about Uncle Tom? I think you got your facts confused and I—

BARRY: You hate Jews. Admit it.

JOHN: No, I don't. Now, I think—

BARRY: I DON'T CARE WHAT YOU THINK. NO ONE DOES! You know why? 'Cause you're trying to kiss my butt, kiss the Master's butt, that's why! You call me up and try to get all empathetic with me about how much you love the Jews and you're lying. You hate them—

JOHN: I don't kiss nobody's butt.

BARRY: Of course you do. You're kissing *my* butt. You're kissing it right now. If you weren't, you'd hang up on me!

JOHN: That's what I'm trying to say. I don't *want* to hang up on you.

BARRY: Then I'll do you the favor. *(x)* "Night Talk," Henry, you're on.

(Linda enters with a pile of fan mail, newspapers, etc. Dumps it all on Barry's desk.)

HENRY: Yeah, hello, Barry?

BARRY: Yessir.

HENRY: Calling from Painesville.

BARRY: Long-distance.

HENRY: I wanted to bring up the topic of the Perry Nuclear Power Plant?

BARRY: Great idea. It'll cut our electric bills in half. You got a problem with that?

HENRY *(Clears his throat)*: "The Perry Nuclear Power Plant is an infringement on the health and well-being of all the people living within a five-hundred-mile radius of its reactor core. We, the members of the Life and Liberty Alliance, protest the building, sale or manufacture of . . ."

BARRY: Wait a minute, wait a minute! Hold on there one second, Henry!

HENRY: ". . . nuclear and nuclear-related materials for any purpose, whether for armaments or so-called peaceful . . ."

BARRY: Hey. Are you reading that? Stu, is he reading that?

HENRY: ". . . utilization that endangers the life of millions of people in the Great Lakes region, specifically, the city of Cleveland . . ."

BARRY: Hey, shut up for a second! ARE YOU READING THAT?!

HENRY: That is our manifesto.

BARRY: I don't care if it's the Magna Carta, you don't read anything over the air on my show. Now you got something to say, say it in your own words or you're off.

HENRY: Look, Barry, the use of nuclear energy is as irresponsible as nuclear war. We feel—

BARRY: Oh, now it's nuclear *war*! I thought you were talking about a power plant. How about toxic waste? That bothers you too, I bet? What about baby seals? Panda bears?

HENRY: That has nothing to do with our protest.

BARRY: We got another panda bear lover here.

HENRY: We're talking about poison. The world's condemning itself to a nuclear doomsday. Our children—

BARRY: Cut it, Henry, all right? What are you telling us? That we're all gonna die? I got news for you, pal, we all die sooner or later. A nuclear war would probably be the best thing to ever happen to the American people. Wake 'em up!

HENRY: I don't know how you can joke about nuclear war! This is—

BARRY: Who says I'm *joking*, pal? Hey, I did my protest bit back in the sixties. I been there, man. Smoking pot. Marching around with the beads and headbands, protesting anything I can think of. Crying about how mean Mommy and Daddy are to me. It was fun. But it was a long time ago. GROW UP, HENRY! Why don't you stop whining and start doing something constructive with your time?

HENRY: That's exactly what I am doing! I'm doing something constructive. Which is more—

BARRY: Shut up for a second! You had your say, now lemme have mine. You're just a spoiled, spineless little baby. Crying about what an unfair world this is. You're a *victim*! You have a victim mentality. Stop smokin' the Mary Jane and face the facts. Yes, nuclear war is a very great possibility. And, yes, Henry, it's scary. And, yes, we don't like it. But all the weepy pseudo-intellectuals in the world aren't going to change things one bit!

HENRY: Your attitude is immoral.

BARRY: Oh, did I hurt your feelings, pal? Go tell it to your shrink.

HENRY: WHEN THAT PLANT EXPLODES AND KILLS TEN THOU-SAND PEOPLE IT WILL BE ON YOUR HEAD!

BARRY: Too bad you can't keep up an intelligent conversation in a normal tone of voice. *(x)* Bob . . . how's tricks?

BOB: Barry, my friend.

BARRY: Bob, what a relief. How you doing tonight?

BOB: Terrific. Very well. Thank you. How are you?

BARRY: Pretty well. Pretty well.

BOB: Congratulations!

BARRY: Thank you.

BOB: I hope you're not gonna get too busy to take my calls.

BARRY: Bob, no show is complete without your call.

BOB: Hee-hee!

BARRY: How are the legs?

BOB: Oh, they're fine. An ache or two, but not bad. You know what I say: "When they give you lemons, make lemonade!"

BARRY: "You can't cry over spilt milk."

BOB: "Cry and you cry alone."

BARRY: Because "you can't lose what you never had."

BOB: Because "you don't know what you've got till you've lost it."

BARRY: "So don't lose hope, this too shall pass."

BOB: Because "today is the first day of the rest of your life."

BARRY: Yeah, and "it's always darkest before dawn." Bob, can I just—

BOB: Because "tomorrow never comes!"

BARRY: Yeah, and "if you play with fire you're gonna get burnt." Bob, can I say something, please?

BOB: Of course, Barry.

BARRY: Thank you. We are all inspired by your courage. You are a brave man and an example to all of us. As they say, Bob, the hero and the coward both feel fear. The difference is that the coward runs away. You didn't run away. And we thank you for that.

BOB: Well, thank you, Barry. But you know, people think that life in a wheelchair must be the worst thing in the world. That's not the way I look at it. I imagine the worst thing in the world would be to be ungrateful for all the good things that come our way every day: the smiles of little children, flowers blooming, the little birds chirping, sitting on the budding branches on a bright spring day! Hell, just seeing the sun coming up every day is a miracle!

BARRY: I couldn't agree with you more, Bob. Especially the part about the little birds. You know I think we get too bogged down in our daily trouble, we forget about the simple things.

BOB: Oh, and I left out one more thing to be thankful for.

BARRY: What's that?

BOB: "Night Talk with Barry Champlain."

BARRY: Thank you, Bob . . . us both being vets, it means a lot to me that you would say that.

BOB: I mean it.

BARRY: I know you do. Look we gotta move along. Be well.

BOB: Oh no!

BARRY: Sorry, gotta run! I know you can't, but we can.

BOB: OK then . . . good luck with that kid.

BARRY: Who?

BOB: The one on drugs there? I hope he calls back.

BARRY: Me, too! Look, Bob? "Don't put all your eggs in one basket."

BOB: "And a bird in hand . . ."

BARRY: G'night, Bob. *(x)* And we have Chet. Chet, so nice to have you back. Shouldn't you be out burning crosses or cleaning your gun collection?

CHET: Just wanted to check in.

BARRY: Good.

CHET: See if you got the package I sent down the station.

BARRY: "Package"?

(In the midst of Barry's fan mail pile protrudes a shoe-box-sized package wrapped in brown paper.)

CHET: You got it. I know you did.

BARRY: You sent me a present, Chet?

CHET: Couldn't decide whether to use a timer or not. Guess you'll have to find out when you open it—

BARRY: Oh wait a minute! Chet! You're not saying you sent me a *bomb*!

CHET: Wrapped in brown paper. I know you're looking at it right now. Just take some C-4, roll it in a pile of nuts and bolts and nails, and it does the job—

BARRY: Wow, what a recipe! You should have your own cooking show, Chet! Sounds very interesting. Didn't get it though. You sure you sent it to the right address? Spell all the words correctly?

CHET: *You* got it.

BARRY: You trying to frighten me, Chet, is that it?

CHET: If I were you I'd have my pretty assistant/slash/producer/slash/whore give the police a call. Take the bomb squad about ten minutes to get down to the station.

BARRY: Bomb squad? Why would I want to call the bomb squad, Chet? Because some pinheaded, anti-Semitic moron calls me and tells me I have a bomb in my mail?

CHET: He who laughs last—

BARRY *(x)*: Oh, shut up. "Night Talk," Denise.

DENISE: I'm scared, Barry.

BARRY: What are you scared of, babe?

DENISE: Nothing specifically, but on the other hand . . . you know, it's like everywhere I go.

BARRY: Yeah?

DENISE: Well, like, Barry, you know, like we've got a garbage disposal in our sink in the kitchen, I mean, my mother's kitchen . . .

BARRY: Um-hmmmmm.

DENISE: And sometimes a teaspoon will fall into the garbage disposal?

(Stu speaks over Denise's monologue into the in-studio mike.)

STU: What you want to do, Barry?

(Barry ignores him, intrigued by the package.)

DENISE: So, like, you know how you feel when you have to reach down . . . into that gunk and you have to feel around down there for that teaspoon? Who knows what's down there? Could be garbage, a piece of something, so much stuff goes down there . . . or germs, which you can't even see.

(As Denise goes on, Barry takes off his headphones and fiddles with the package, to the horror of everyone in the station.)

If they're gonna be anywhere, they're gonna be down that disposal. They grow there, see? They come back up the pipes. Salmonella, yeast, viruses, flu, even cancer, who knows? But, Barry, even without all that, what if, and I'm just saying "what if," what if the garbage disposal came on while your hand was down there?

BARRY: That'd be a handful, wouldn't it?

DENISE: I get so scared of thinking about it that I usually leave the teaspoon down there. I don't even try to get it out. But then I'm afraid that my mother will get mad if she finds it down there, so I turn the disposal on, trying to make it go down the drain. But all it does is make a huge racket. And I stand in the middle of the kitchen and the spoon goes around and around, and I get sort of paralyzed, you know? It makes a lot of noise, because I know the teaspoon is getting destroyed and annihilated and that's good 'cause I hate that teaspoon for scaring me like that . . .

BARRY: Denise! Lemme get this straight. You're afraid of the garbage disposal in your mother's kitchen?

DENISE: Well, it's not just the garbage disposal, it's everything. What about insects? Termites. Hornets . . .

(During the call, the booths behind Barry are abuzz with activity regarding the "bomb" on Barry's desk. Dan is on the phone. Linda enters Barry's studio.)

BARRY: Tell Dan the mail is my business!

LINDA: This is not funny! You're such an asshole.

BARRY *(Into in-studio mike, to Dan)*: You better not be on the phone calling the police. Hang up that phone or I walk! I said hang up or I'm outta here. I'm not kidding!

DENISE: . . . Spiders. Ants. Centipedes. Bedbugs. Roaches. Mites. You can't even see mites. They're like the germs. Tiny, impossible to see! I like things to be clean. Dirty ashtrays bother me . . .

(Dan hangs up. Barry continues to investigate the box.)

Just one more unknown. Just like the houses on our street. Used to be we knew who lived on our street. But that was years ago. Now all kinds of different people live on our street. Foreigners. People with accents. What are they doing on our street? What are their habits? Are they clean? Are they sanitary?

BARRY: Why don't you ask one of them?

(Barry opens the box. Inside is a dead rat, which he picks up by the tail and flips onto his desk. Beneath that, a large Nazi flag. He flaunts it before Dan and the others watching through the plate glass.)

DENISE: Oh sure. That would be a great idea to just go to somebody's house and knock on the door. Who knows who's behind that door? Maybe a serial murderer? What if Ted Bundy or the Boston Strangler was living there, just sitting inside watching television, and I came to the door? Great! Come on in, Denise! That's why I don't go to strange people's houses anymore. I keep the doors locked at all times. But that isn't going to solve anything. You're not going to stop a plane from crashing into your house, now are you?

BARRY: No.

DENISE: The mailman brings me unsolicited mail, I mean, the postage stamp could have been licked by someone with AIDS. Right? My mother is a threat to my life just by persisting to go out there . . . Barry, did you know that there's this dust storm in California that has these fungus spores in it? And these spores get into people's lungs, and it goes into their bloodstreams and grows inside them and kills them! Strange air . . . strange air . . . you have to . . . Oh! There's my mother. She'll kill me if she finds out I used the phone! *(x)*

(Pause.)

BARRY: "Strange air." That's what we've got for you tonight. I think I see the station manager, Dan Woodruff, lurking in the corner warning me that if I don't wedge in a word from our sponsors he's gonna do something outrageous like remove his toupee. Don't wanna have that happen . . . So lemme tell you where to eat . . .

DAN *(Entering Barry's studio):* Barry . . .

BARRY: Linda, coffee please?

DAN: I had the police on the line.

BARRY: Why?

DAN: You know why. Do you have any idea—

BARRY: Dan, go home, you're cramping my style.

DAN: Barry . . .

BARRY: Stu, check your level on line three. I'm getting a buzz . . .

DAN: Barry, I need ten seconds of your time . . .

BARRY: OK, Dan.

DAN: That kid who called, the one on drugs with the girlfriend.

BARRY: "Kent." Yeah?

DAN: "Kent" . . . is a problem. I just got a call from Metroscan and they're kind of anxious about this kid. Think you should have done something a little more concrete.

BARRY: What do you want me to say? It's a hoax, Dan. There's no girlfriend. I get calls like this all the time.

DAN: They don't know that.

BARRY: Who doesn't?

DAN: Metroscan, Barry. The people who are going to put you on the air coast to coast . . .

BARRY: You're consulting with these . . . "suits" now on how to run my show?

DAN: Don't do this to me.

BARRY: Do what, Dan? It's done. The kid's history.

DAN: We can't trace the call or something?

BARRY: "Trace the call"?

DAN: I'm just saying—

BARRY: Stu, trace the call. Find the kid.

STU: I don't think—

BARRY: Just do it. Happy, Dan?

DAN: Thank you, Barry. That's great. You're the best. Oh . . . and what if it isn't a hoax? What if the girl is dead?

BARRY: We'll send her a wreath.

(Dan moves to the control booths.)

STU: Harry's Restaurant. Runs long.

(Barry slips on his headset, and sensing the ad is over, jumps onto his mike.)

BARRY: Wait a minute, before I take any more callers, I have to say something . . . Isn't that the most sickening ad copy you've ever heard? Harry's Restaurant? Home cooking? You ever go back into the kitchen of that joint, you'd think you were in a taco stand in Tijuana. That was a pretaped spot you just listened to, something the sponsors force me to do. They like to make Barry sound homey and candid. Well, here's candid—the ad makes me wanna puke. Which I usually do right after I eat at Harry's . . . "Night Talk," June.

JUNE: Hello?

BARRY: Hello.

JUNE: Hello, am I on?

BARRY: You're on.

JUNE: Oh, Barry, I wanted to say something about the people who don't pick up after their doggies when they take them for a walk. My Buttons is only a toy poodle so all I have to carry with me is a little garden spade. I would think some people need a snow shovel.

BARRY: Yeah, that's a pretty disgusting topic there, June.

JUNE: It is. It is. But, Barry, that young man who was having a drug overdose. Is he going to die? Eh?

BARRY: We all die, June.

JUNE: Uh-huh. Tell me, Barry, do you have a doggie?

BARRY: I own no pets.

JUNE: What's that?

BARRY: No pets allowed in the Champlain compound. No dogs, no cats, no mice, no goldfish, no gerbils. I own no pets.

JUNE: Oh, but you have to have a pet. How can you live without a pet, Barry, eh?

BARRY: Well, I'll tell you, June. When I was a kid my father gave me a golden Lab for my tenth birthday. Beautiful dog. Very friendly. All the kids loved her.

JUNE: Oh yes, they're lovely doggies . . . lovely . . .

BARRY: We used to go for long walks through the woods . . . Goldie, that was her name, Goldie . . .

JUNE: Like Goldie Hawn . . . what a nice name!

BARRY: Yeah, well one day, we were out walking in the woods. Beautiful autumn day. The leaves were just changing on the trees. We came out along this highway. Goldie saw a male German shepherd on the other side, didn't look where she was going, ran across the road . . . got hit dead-on by a Greyhound bus doing around ninety . . .

JUNE: Did she die?

BARRY: Of course she died, June. She was dragged for about a quarter mile.

JUNE: Awwww.

BARRY: Thought that was kind of ironic, you know, dog getting hit by a Greyhound bus. I could never bring myself to get another one after that. You never know what might happen . . . to your dog. Especially the small ones, the toy poodles for instance, like yours. Always getting their heads caught in slamming doors or falling down garbage disposals. Or sometimes, when you're busy talking on the phone, they get all wrapped up in that plastic that comes with the dry cleaning. And they're all caught up in that stuff, yapping and suffocating, and you can't hear them 'cause you're too busy talking on the phone. You know what I'm saying? June? June? June? Guess she had to go walk her doggie. Listen to this . . .

(An ad begins to play as Barry moves to the control booths. Linda steps forward and addresses the audience:)

LINDA: One night after work, about two years ago, I stopped by the lunchroom. I was thirsty. I was gonna get a Coke out of the machine. Barry was there, sitting at the crummy table under the crummy fluorescent light. I didn't know him. I had been working here in the news department two months, and in that whole time he hadn't said more than three words to me. He was sitting there, alone, staring at this ashtray full of butts. Just sitting and staring.

I asked him if anything was wrong. He looked up at me like he'd never seen me before. Like he had no idea where he was. He said, "I'm outta cigarettes." I said, "There's a machine down the hall. I'll get you some." I mean, he coulda gotten the cigarettes himself, I knew that, but at that particular moment it seemed like he couldn't. When I brought him the cigs, he gazed up at me with this tremendous look of gratitude. And then he said, "Linda? Can I go home with you tonight? Can I sleep with you?" Now I've had a lot of guys come on to me in a lot of interesting ways. And I was expecting this Barry guy to have a smooth approach, but this angle was unexpectedly unique.

I didn't say, "Yes," I didn't say, "No." We went to this diner and I watched him eat a bacon cheeseburger. He was talking about something, what was it? Oh yeah, *euthanasia*! I remember, because the whole time he's going on, I'm thinking this guy really knows how to sweet-talk a girl.

Of course, we ended up at my place. As I was making us drinks, I said to myself, Linda, you know you're going to go to bed with this guy, so let's get the show on the road.

He was so nervous. Like he was going to jump out of his skin. I gave him a shoulder massage. Finally he makes a move and we're on the floor rolling around. He's kissing me like he's a drowning man trying to get onto a life raft!

I got us into the bedroom. Then I go into the bathroom for two seconds to get myself together, and, anyway, when I get back to the bed, he's asleep, curled up in a ball. All that night, while he slept, he's throwin' himself around, tossing and turning, grinding his teeth, clenching his fists. It was disturbing.

Next morning, I wake up to the smell of toast and coffee. I hear the shower running. He's been up for two hours, making us breakfast, reading the paper, who knows what. He comes out of the shower, says he never slept so well. Then he drops his towel, slips into bed and we . . . made love.

Since then, we've spent maybe a dozen nights together. Lemme put it this way—Barry Champlain is a nice place to visit, but I wouldn't want to live there.

(Barry returns to his console. He slips on his headset, gets ready.)

BARRY *(Into in-studio mike)*: Hey, Stu, is that the kid on line three?

STU: Yeah. Kent. He just called back.

LINDA: Don't take that call.

BARRY: Why not?

LINDA: You don't need it.

BARRY: Stu?

STU: I think he's lyin'. You know it. I know it.

BARRY: Dan wants it. Metroscan wants it.

LINDA: Please don't.

BARRY: You find the Miles?

STU: Locked and loaded.

BARRY: Hit me. *(Miles Davis's* Kind of Blue *is heard, soft and mellow. Back on the air)* I don't know about you folks, but I'm feeling kinda blue. You'll never guess who we've got back. That's right, a young man who likes to party just a little too much. Hello, Kent.

KENT: I didn't mean to hang up on you.

BARRY: But you did.

KENT: Yeah . . . I—

BARRY: Kent, you're a fake. A hoax. You cook up some fake-o story about how you and your girlfriend are taking drugs . . .

KENT: We were—

BARRY: . . . and she's OD'd and your parents are in Acapulco.

KENT: Fiji.

BARRY: What?! Fiji. An important detail. And you're just this mixed-up kid who doesn't have a clue about what to do.

KENT: It's true—

BARRY: I don't buy it, Kent.

KENT: Well, there's no way to prove it to you—

BARRY: Sure there is. Give Stu your address and we'll send someone over there.

KENT: You?

BARRY: No, not me, Kent.

KENT: But—

BARRY: Kent, you got people in my audience thinking something bad really happened. You have everyone all upset. Your girlfriend . . . what's her name?

KENT: Uh, Jill.

BARRY: OK, "Jill." Jill has what . . . OD'd?

(Dan watches Barry through the plate glass.)

KENT: I don't know . . . I can't get her to wake up—

BARRY: Yeah. Right. OK. We heard that already. You were smokin' crack and she won't wake up. OK. Let's run with this, why not? Just for kicks, is she *breathing*?

KENT: I'll go check . . .

BARRY *(Into in-studio mike)*: Oh, I can't believe this. Stu, why am I talking to this guy?

STU: Because you're wise and humane?

BARRY: No. That's not it. It's my morbid curiosity. Some dark force compels me to listen to this garbage.

KENT: Yeah, she's breathin'. I think. It's hard to tell . . . There's some, like, foam coming out of her mouth.

BARRY *(Back on the air)*: What!

KENT: There's foam coming out of her mouth . . .

(Linda moves to the control booths.)

BARRY: Is it kinda blue?

KENT: Huh? What?

BARRY: All right, all right. I've had enough of this crap. You and I both know you're lying. I'm cutting you off. Get off my show!

KENT: No, wait!

BARRY: That's it.

KENT: LISTEN! My parents ARE in Fiji! And we were partying . . . But, uh . . . the stuff about my girlfriend . . .

BARRY: Hm-hmm.

KENT: She . . .

BARRY: Come on, Kent, spit it out!

KENT: You'll hang up on me!

BARRY: I won't.

KENT: You promise?

BARRY: I promise I won't hang up on you.

KENT: I made the whole thing up. *(Stoner laugh)*

BARRY *(Glancing at Dan)*: Kent?

KENT: What?

BARRY: I lied—I'm cutting you off.

KENT: NO! NO! PLEASE!

BARRY: Sayonara. Good-bye.

KENT: Please! Please! I'm not lying now! I gotta talk to you . . . Please.

BARRY: You gotta talk to me? About what? Your mother just slit her wrists and she's bleeding to death? How about your father? What's . . . he got a shotgun in his mouth? Gonna blow his brains out? Who else is dead, Kent?

KENT: No one's dead.

BARRY: Come on, who's dead? Who's dead?

KENT: No one's dead!

BARRY: Then we have nothing else to talk about.

KENT: You're making me nervous. I just want to talk.

BARRY: Not tonight, Kent.

KENT: But . . . wait, wait! You're making me all nervous. I just want to *talk*.

BARRY: OK, Kent. Let's talk.

KENT: I listen all the time. I think about what you say. You say such cool stuff, and I thought if I, you know, made an impression . . . maybe I could, you know, meet you.

BARRY: You're goofing again, Kent. You wanted to "meet me"? You can meet me anytime you want. I'm right here at the station.

KENT: At the station?

BARRY: I'm not the president, for God's sake. I'm just some guy on the radio. I'm right here. Downtown. In Terminal Tower. In the studio.

KENT: So I could just come down? . . .

BARRY: You could just come down.

KENT: Now?

BARRY: Now?

KENT: Right now?

BARRY: What do you mean, "right now?"

KENT: Right now . . . could I come down and meet you. Right now!!

BARRY: I'm on the air, Kent.

KENT: PLEASE!!!!!

(Barry glances at Dan, who shakes his head no.)

BARRY: Uh, sure, Kent. Why not? Come on down, I'd love to meet you.

KENT: Really? Really? Great!

BARRY: Just hurry it up, we're already halfway through the show.

KENT: Wait. Wait. I'll be right down! *(x)*

(Theme music.)

BARRY: We're at the end of the first hour of exciting and intellectual conversation. Don't go away. We have news and weather coming up, and then we'll be back with more "Night Talk." I'm Barry Champlain.

(News and weather plays under. Dan and Linda enter Barry's studio.)

DAN: Barry.

BARRY: Linda, call security and let them know this kid is coming . . . Dan, you want anything? Coffee, tea, insulin, crack? We have it all right here.

DAN: Barry, the kid's not coming on this show and that's it. We have too much riding on what's happening tonight.

BARRY: What's happening tonight?

DAN: If they sense for one second you are out of control . . .

BARRY: That's just it, Dan, I *am* out of control. That's the whole point. That's why they're buying the show. *My* show. If I want to have this kid on my show, I'll have him on the show. I put who I want on *my* show. That's why I've got the ratings, Dan. If I want to bring serial killers on this show, I will do it. Charlie Manson. I want Charlie Manson on, he's coming on. Or John Wayne Gacy. Sirhan Sirhan. Or how 'bout this, Dan?

I get David Berkowitz, Bernard Goetz and John Hinckley on, we do a special on GUN CONTROL! What was the name of that guy in San Diego who shot up the McDonald's?

LINDA: Huberty?

BARRY: That's it. Huberty! James Huberty. We get James Huberty and that Texas tower guy, Charles Whitman—make a great show, Dan! See, you have to *think* about these things, Dan. You have to think big! What ever happened to Richard Speck? And the nurses? Let's bring them on the show! Fly them in from Chicago! Think about it, Dan, think! I gotta go take a piss.

(Barry starts to leave, then comes back.)

Wait! I got it! That postman from Oklahoma! He killed four-teen people, Dan. He killed his *boss*! We bring him in, do a special on employees who kill their bosses and we bring *you* on as a guest! That's it, that's what we gotta do! Give the people what they want!

(Barry moves to the control booths. Linda follows. Dan, like Stu and Linda before him, addresses the audience:)

DAN: Mantovani. Burt Bacharach. Mancini. The Jackie Gleason Orchestra. They call it "easy listening," "beautiful music." Serene—melodic—repellent. The kind of shit you hear on elevators. The kind of shit this station played between 1967 and 1980.

When they hired me, this station was in a financial black hole—a huge sucking drain—because they were getting killed by the likes of the Rolling Stones and Grand Funk Railroad. I turned the whole thing upside down. I said: "Screw the music, how 'bout an all-talk station?" My idea—all talk, all the time. I rounded up the best sports commentator, the best financial guy, a psychologist, a home handyman and a sweet, old guy the ladies loved to chat with. I had myself a full deck. But I was missing my ace of spades—or should I say "my joker."

Then I heard Barry Champlain, a wild man down in Akron. Liked to get people wound up, take calls, argue. Hang up on people.

Went down to see him. Over lunch, I laid out my plan. I would hire him. But before he arrived in Cleveland, we would do a make-over. I looked over his résumé. Saw he had been stationed at Fort Dix for six months in 1969, got discharged for a hernia or something like that. So I turned him into a Vietnam vet. I asked him if he ever smoked pot. He said he did, maybe once or twice, so I turned him into a hardcore hippie too. Barry Champlain marched in all the antiwar marches after he saw the horrors of war in Southeast Asia, of course. Before that he had pitched minor league ball for the Toledo Mudhens. I gave him a pilot's license, had him living alone in a tent in the Yukon for a year, and—oh, I'm particularly proud of this one—he got a Ph.D. in history from the University of Chicago after writing a book on Martin Luther and the Reformation. A true Renaissance man.

I laid this all out to him over lunch. He sat there, chewing his tuna fish sandwich. I could almost see the gears turning in his head. Then I hit him with the closer, the name of the show: "Night Talk with Barry Champlain"—his name would be fifty percent of the show's title. He stopped chewing. I had my joker.

Like trains in and out of a train station, talent comes and goes.

(Barry reenters his studio. Sits, checks his notes.)

You miss one, here comes another. There'll always be another train. And trains wear out, they get derailed. They crash. Sooner or later they're out of commission. One thing for sure, the faster they go, the harder they crash.

Barry's my train. I put him on the track, I keep him on the track. I keep him oiled and on the track. I let him go as fast as he can. The faster the better.

This is a great job. I enjoy myself every day. It's just about perfect. You get into trouble when you forget it's a job. You get into trouble when you start thinking you're doing something more. It'll fuck you up every time.

But that's Barry's problem. Not mine. *(Returns to the control booths)*

BARRY: "Night Talk." We're back now with Vincent.

VINCENT: I been listening to you for five years.

BARRY: Yeah?

VINCENT: The guys here at the store put you on every night. We laugh our asses off.

BARRY: Thank you.

VINCENT: We can't get over what a jerk-off and a loser you are!

BARRY *(x):* "Night Talk." Agnes?

AGNES: Barry, can I ask you a question?

BARRY: Hit me, babe.

AGNES: Oh, I wouldn't hit you for the world. *I Love Lucy.* Why don't they make more of 'em?

BARRY: What?

AGNES: The *I Love Lucy* show. It's so good, why don't they make more of 'em? I feel like I've seen each one at least ten times. Don't you think they should make some new ones?

BARRY: Those shows are ancient, Agnes! Lucille Ball is an old woman! And the rest of the cast is dead.

AGNES: No, she's not! I saw her on the show the other night. She looked to be around thirty-five! And that Ricky Ricardo, he could play my bongos any day!

BARRY: Let me ask you something, Agnes. Do you know what year this is?

AGNES: Wait a second, let me look . . .

BARRY *(x):* "Night Talk," Chris!

CHRIS: Good evening, Barry.

BARRY: Yeah?

CHRIS: Some people think God is dead. Do you think God is dead, Barry?

BARRY: I happen to know that God is alive and well and living in Gary, Indiana. He's a black steelworker with seven kids who works the night shift pouring off slag.

CHRIS: I see. *(Pause)* But, Barry, do you believe in God?

BARRY: Are we being serious here, Chris?

CHRIS: I'm serious. I think it's very important.

BARRY: And why is it important what I believe? Can't you think for yourself?

CHRIS: Don't you think that without some kind of belief in God our actions in this world are meaningless? It would just be physics and chemicals without God . . . just shapes and colors . . .

BARRY: Shapes and colors? Come on! Chris! We been reading William Blake?

CHRIS: I think you do believe in God.

BARRY: Oh, you do.

CHRIS: Yes, you believe in God. It's simple. You think you *are* God. And aren't you ashamed? *(x)*

BARRY: On that note, let's hear from our sponsors. Hope you stick around for the second coming. *(Into in-studio mike)* What are you doing to me, Stu? You're killing me, you're killing me right on the fucking air. Fuck! Fuck me! This is not the night to fuck up like this, Stu!

(Linda ushers Kent into Barry's studio.)

Wait, don't tell me. Let me guess . . .

LINDA: He seems harmless.

BARRY: Yeah, baboons seem harmless.

LINDA: You sit over here, Kent. This is your microphone, speak directly into it, keeping your mouth about six inches away. Remember the ground rules: no brand names, no last names, no phone numbers over the air. Otherwise, speak and act naturally. This is Mr. Champlain.

KENT: This is great! You're Barry?

BARRY: You got 'im . . .

KENT: Wow. *(Just stares at Barry)*
BARRY: What's wrong with him?
LINDA: I think he's starstruck.
STU: We're going in five . . . four . . . three . . .
BARRY: OK, pal, we're on.

(Theme music.)

We're back. With me right now is a very special guest: Kent.
Say hi to everyone, Kent.
KENT: Wow.
BARRY: My sentiments exactly. We've brought Kent on board to give
us an intimate look at the future of America. Kent is the clas-
sic American youth: energetic and resourceful, spoiled, per-
verse and disturbed . . . would you say that's an accurate
description, Kent?
KENT: Yeah, sure.
BARRY: What do you call that haircut?
KENT: I dunno. Punk?
BARRY: Are you high right now, Kent?
KENT: High?
BARRY: Are you on drugs? Or is this just your naturally moronic self?
Wipe the drool off your mouth, you're getting the desk all
wet.
KENT: I can't believe I'm here, man. Does this really work?
BARRY: This is a radio station, Kent. You're sitting in front of a live
mike. When you speak, thousands of people can hear your
voice. It penetrates their minds.

*(Kent leans into his mike and screams a rock yowl. Everyone in the
studio tears off their headsets.)*

KENT: Wanna send that one out to Diamond Dave and Billy the bass
player and all the babes at the Horizon mall!
BARRY: Kent, we're discussing America here tonight. You have any
thoughts on that subject?

KENT: America . . . is a country . . .

BARRY: That's a good start.

KENT: It's where the revolution was. It's the home of democracy, like you were saying before . . .

BARRY: Go on . . . uh-huh . . .

KENT: That's how come we can have, you know, interesting talk shows and TV and stuff. Because there's freedom in America. I wouldn't wanna live in Russia, you know, because they don't have any freedom. And their TV shows *suck*. I heard all they have is news. I mean, the news here sucks, too. All they ever talk about is Nicaragua and Iran. All these boring places filled with boring people. Who cares, you know? How come they never talk about cool places like London or Lauderdale or Antarctica?

BARRY: Or Fiji? You forgot Fiji, Kent.

KENT: What? Yeah.

BARRY: Oh, I'm sorry I broke your train of thought. Keep going. This is exhilarating.

KENT: Well, nobody talks about what the kids are into. Skateboarding. Or music.

BARRY: You find politics boring.

KENT: Oh, nah, man! I'm very political. That Live Aids concert was pretty good. You know. Hands Across America. And I like Bruce, and he's political.

BARRY: Bruce? Bruce Springsteen? Yeah, a very deep political thinker. He's a communist, isn't he?

KENT: Nah, man, he's from New Jersey. His babe's awesome.

BARRY: Whose babe?

KENT: Bruce's!

BARRY: Oh, Mr. Springsteen's wife!

KENT: *Julianne.* She was a model. All the rock stars go with models. Keith and Patti. Mick and Jerry. Prince . . . and . . . That's the way it works. The models hang out with the guys they think are the coolest and they want to make it with them. The stars.

BARRY: You've studied this.

KENT: You know what I'm talking about, Barry. Look at you, big star, famous guy, and you've got that fine fox right over there that works for you. Models. *So* . . . if you've got some cash, and you're cool, you get to have a model.

BARRY: What about Stu? Does he get to have a model?

KENT: Stu? Nah, man. Women are looking for the alpha male. I saw a show about it on TV. The top gorilla, he makes it with all the babe gorillas!

BARRY: So you're not into women's liberation?

KENT: No, man, I am! I am! I'm into everybody getting liberated. Women. South Africans. All the people of the world. I saw a show about all that stuff. Revolution is pretty important, you know? There's gonna be more and more revolutions. Then the people are going to get together—SOLIDARITY—against the system! Like that song by Megadeth: "Peace Sells . . . But Who's Buying?" "Peace Sells . . . But Who's Buying?" Plus . . . plus . . . there was this movie I saw about how people will have two-way TVs so they can see each other, and then they won't be able to *stop* the revolution . . .

BARRY: *Who* won't be able to stop it?

KENT: Big Brother! The Government! Corporations! They're all fascists, man—wanna control everybody's mind. Make us into zombies. But freedom's an important thing, like you always say, Barry. You say the best things. That's why I listen to you every single day. Because you know what you're talking about. You're great.

(Beat.)

BARRY: Kent, you're an idiot. I sincerely hope you do not represent the future of this country, because if you do we are in sad shape.

KENT: Barry. You're so funny! That's why I love to listen to your show. All the kids listen. You're the best thing on the radio.

BARRY: Kent, America is waiting for you and your friends, indeed the world is. The future looks difficult in this country. What are you planning to do about the armaments race? Toxic wastes? Organized crime? The looming energy crisis? The breakdown

of the political system? How are you going to prepare for the
future?

KENT: First thing I'm going to do . . .

BARRY: Yes?

KENT: Is tune in to "Night Talk with Barry Champlain" Mondays
through Fridays on W-T-L-K!!!

BARRY: That's pretty funny. You're a funny guy, like to party, have
fun. Am I part of your good time?

KENT: You know it, bro!

BARRY: Kent, we discuss a lot of disturbing subjects on this show.
Tragic things. Frightening things. Doesn't *any* of that bother
you?

KENT: Nope.

BARRY: Why not?

KENT: It's just a show!

BARRY: Just one big rock video, eh?

KENT: Yeah, Barry . . . you know . . . it's *your* show!

BARRY: Yeah. That it is. That . . . it . . . is. My show. Well, let's get
back to the callers on *my* show.

KENT: Sure thing, Bar!

BARRY: Julia.

JULIA: Barry, hello, yes. I think these people who have been calling
in tonight are a bunch of I-don't-know-whats! It's crazy. And
that crazy kid you got on there. It's terrible. I've been listening to you for *five* years straight, Barry, and I love you and
your show. I think it's terrific that more folks are going to be listening. I just hope you have time for your long-time friends.

BARRY: Always have time for my friends, Julia.

JULIA: You're terrific. And your show's terrific, and I don't know what
else to say.

BARRY: Well, tell me something, Julia, since you listen all the time.
What is it that you like about the show?

JULIA: Well, I don't know . . . a lot of things.

BARRY: Like what, for example?

JULIA: Well, I love *you*, Bar.

BARRY: Yeah, that's a given. OK, what about me do you love?

JULIA: Well, you're very funny.

BARRY: Uh-huh . . .

JULIA: And I love to hear you talk about all the things you have to say.

BARRY: OK, OK. Then let's get back to the show. The show must serve some kind of purpose for you.

JULIA: No, I wouldn't say that.

BARRY: What would you say?

JULIA: Well, I don't know . . .

BARRY: What do you mean, you don't know? You've said that at least five times now! What don't you know? You've been listening to this show for five years and you don't know *why* you listen to it?

JULIA: I just said . . .

BARRY: I heard what you said. You said you don't know why you listen. Lemme tell you why you listen. You listen so you can feel superior to the other losers who call in.

JULIA: Barry!

BARRY: Don't "Barry" me! You're a dimwit. Instead of brains you've got sawdust between your ears. Just listen to you. If I sounded half as stupid as you do, I'd be too embarrassed to open my mouth!

JULIA: I'm hanging up.

BARRY: Good. Don't call back. *(x)*

KENT: Wow.

BARRY: Nothing more boring than people who love you. "Night Talk." You're on.

CALLER: I just have one thing to ask you, Barry.

BARRY: Hit me.

CALLER: Are you as ugly as you sound?

BARRY: Uglier.

(Linda can be seen picking up a phone in one of the control booths.)

CALLER: Yeah, I thought you'd say something like that. As usual, you avoid the question.

BARRY: What's the question?

CALLER: I think you know the question.

BARRY: Is it animal, vegetable or mineral?

CALLER: The question is obvious, why does an intelligent fellow like yourself spend so much energy hurting other people? Don't you love yourself? I think you must be the loneliest person—

BARRY *(x)*: "Night Talk," Allan.

ALLAN: You love to cut people off, Champlain. You wanna push folks around. You know why? 'Cause you're a sorry mother. You're a failure. That jerk kid is making a jackass out of you.

BARRY *(x)*: "Night Talk," Cheryl Ann.

LINDA *(As Cheryl Ann)*: I'm confused, Barry.

BARRY: What did you say your name was?

LINDA: Cheryl Ann.

(Barry glances over at the control booth where Linda is making the "Cheryl Ann" call. She keeps her back to him. Kent is oblivious.)

BARRY: OK, "Cheryl Ann." What are you confused about?

LINDA: It's about my boyfriend?

BARRY: Your "boyfriend," huh?

LINDA: Actually, this guy I work with. And well, it's funny . . . He drinks too much. Smokes too much. Drugs . . . Never stops driving himself.

BARRY: Sounds like my kind of guy.

LINDA: Yeah. Well, I want to help him . . . with what he's going through . . .

BARRY: Maybe he doesn't want your help.

LINDA: I don't know. I think—

BARRY: You think?

LINDA: I'm . . . It's hard to say this—

BARRY: Yeah, well, we got to move it along here, Cheryl Ann. A lot of callers tonight.

LINDA: OK. Look. I have feelings for this guy.

BARRY: What kind of feelings?

LINDA: Nice feelings—

BARRY: Sexual feelings?

LINDA: Sure. Yes. OK. But see . . . I want him to take me seriously. I want to take care of him. I want him to . . .

BARRY: Listen, Cheryl Ann, sounds like you're barking up the wrong tree. Do yourself a favor, kick this guy out of your life and go get yourself a new vibrator. *(x)* "Night Talk," Ralph.

RALPH: They asked me: "Why did you do it? Why are you so angry?" They don't understand, Barry, me and you. Barry, we're the kind of people, we *feel* too much.

(Behind the plate glass, Linda is putting on her coat, getting ready to leave the radio station.)

BARRY: Hey, Ralph, we playing with a full deck here or what?

RALPH: I'm not saying I have the answers—who does? I used to think I knew, but now, who knows? Take for instance—take cancer. What is it? A virus? A bacteria? What difference does it make? It kills you just the same. Just as fast. They tell me little babies are starving in Africa. OK. I'll buy that. But where? Exactly where? And what am I suppposed to do about it? See, all I know is me—and me, I'm getting screwed. Barry, they say they're gonna come here and take my TV set and take my refrigerator. What are they gonna do with my TV set?

BARRY: Probably watch it, that's what people do with TV sets.

RALPH: But when they do, what do they see? They see people killing people. Babies starving. Floods. Hurricanes. And for what? For nothing. Beer commercials. Tampax ads. MTV. A diamond earring. I guess so. All I know is what I read in the papers. And that's a lot of talk-talk-talk-talk-talk . . .

BARRY: Ralph-Ralph-Ralph-Ralph-Ralph! Tell me something. I'm curious. How do you dial a phone with a straitjacket on?

RALPH: Sure, I'll listen. I'll listen to common sense. But who's got it anymore? Barry, even if you've got it, you're the only one. Just you and me. Nobody else. Everybody knows God is dead. You know why?

BARRY: Why?

RALPH: 'Cause Lot couldn't keep the Sodomites away from the angels. They were trying to do it with the angels! Lot tried to tell 'em: "Don't do it!" But they wouldn't listen. And now the guy's dead. See what I'm saying? I don't know much about God, I never was very religious, but you can't help feeling something's wrong, like no one's driving the train. The system. Too many people gettin' sick, and the traffic's jammin' up, and even the weather's not been very good lately. I don't get it, Barry, I don't—

KENT *(Jumps onto his mike):* You don't get it, wimp? Here's what you get! You get ninety-nine cents, go down the drugstore, buy yourself a pack of razor blades and slash your fuckin' wrists, pinhead!

BARRY: Let's hear from our sponsors!

(Stu charges into Barry's studio. He grabs Kent.)

STU: OK, pal, back to the mall!

KENT: No!

STU: Come on, Kent. Visit's over.

KENT: No! Wait, I'm not done!

STU: Yes, you are! Barry's done with you.

KENT: Barry! Hey, man, come on! We were just warming up! Right? Barry! BARRY! Don't be that way, man. You know me. Don't do this. BARRY!

(Kent rushes up to Barry. He pulls out something. A gun? He pulls it out fully. It's not a gun. It's a disposable camera. Kent takes a flash picture of Barry, howls like a banshee and then rushes out. Stu chases him. Barry stumbles around, disoriented by all the action. Dan pops into Barry's studio.)

DAN: Barry, I gotta say it. You dispelled any doubts I may have had about the show tonight. They *loved* it! Great choices. Great work. You and the kid . . . Unorthodox show but brilliant. G'night, champ. See you Monday.

(Dan leaves the station.)

STU *(Returning; into in-studio mike)*: Ten seconds, Barry. Spike, keep the ads rolling. We need time here.

(Through the plate glass, Stu watches Barry, who has found his way back to his console, but can't seem to get it together. Stu addresses Barry over the in-studio mike:)

I was thinking maybe we should send out for a bottle for after the show. Whaddyou say? Or maybe hash it out over at the Red Coach. C'mon, Barry, no big deal, it's just one show. Not that important. C'mon, man, you don't like heights—don't climb mountains.

BARRY: Fuck you.

STU: No. Not fuck *me.* Fuck *you.* It's like the kid said—it's your show.

(Stu grabs his jacket and leaves the station. Barry considers leaving as well. He gets up, takes a few steps, then returns once again to his console. He puts on his headset.)

BARRY *(Into in-studio mike)*: Kill it, Spike. *(On the air)* I'm here. I'm here every night, I come up here every night. This is my job, this is what I do for a living. I come up here and I do the best I can. I give you the best I can. I can't do better than this. I can't. I'm only a human being up here. I'm not God. Ummm. A lot of you out there are not . . . I may not be the most popular guy in the world. That's not the point. I really don't care what you think of me. I mean, who the hell are you anyways? *(Beat)* You—audience—you call me up and you try to tell me things about myself. You don't know me. You don't know anything about me. You've never seen me. You don't know what I look like. You don't know who I am. What I want. What I like, what I don't like in this world. I'm just a voice. A voice crying in the wilderness. And you, like a pack of baying wolves, descend on me, because you can't stand facing what it is you are and what you've made. Yes, the world is a terrible place. Yes, cancer and garbage disposals will get you! Yes, a war is coming. Yes, the world is shot to hell and you're all goners. Everything's screwed up and you like it that way, don't you? You're fascinated by the gory details. You're mesmerized by your own fear! You revel in floods and car accidents and terrorist attacks and unstoppable diseases. You're happiest when others are in pain. And that's where I come in, isn't it? I'm here to lead you by the hand through the dark forest of your own hatred and anger and humiliation. I'm providing a public service. You're so *scared*. You're like little children under the covers afraid of the bogeyman, but you can't live without him. Your fear, your own lives have become your entertainment. *(Beat)* Monday night, millions of people are going to be listening to this show. AND YOU HAVE NOTHING TO SAY. NOTHING TO TALK ABOUT. Marvelous technology is at our disposal and instead of reaching up for new heights, we try to see how far down we can go. How deep into the muck we can immerse ourselves. What do you want to talk about? Baseball scores? Your pets? Orgasms? You're pathetic. I despise each and every one of you. You've got nothing. Nothing. Absolutely nothing. No brains. No power. No future. No hope. No God. *(Beat)* The only thing you believe in, is me. What are you, if you don't have me? Because I'm not afraid, see. I come up here every night. And I make my case. I make my point. I say what I believe in. I have to. I have no choice. You frighten me. So I come up here and I try to tell you the truth. I tear into you. I abuse you. I insult you. And you just keep calling. Why do you keep coming back? What's wrong with you? I don't want to hear any more. I've had enough. Stop talking. Don't call anymore. Go away. Bunch of yellow-bellied, spineless, bigoted, quivering, drunken, insomniatic, paranoid, disgusting, perverted, voyeuristic, little obscene phone callers. That's what you are. *(Beat)* Well to hell with ya . . . I don't need your fear and your stupidity. You don't get it. It's wasted on you. Pearls before swine! *(Beat)* If just one person out there had any idea what I'm talking about! . . . Fred, you're on.

FRED: Yes . . . you see . . . Barry . . . I know it's depressing that so many people don't understand that you're just joking—

BARRY *(x):* Jackie, you're on!

JACKIE: I've been listening for many years and I find you a warm and intelligent voice in the—

BARRY *(x):* Debbie, you're on!

DEBBIE: Stan called. He told me he never wants to see me again!—

BARRY *(x):* Arnold.

ARNOLD: What you were saying before about loneliness. I'm an electrical engineer and—

BARRY *(x):* Lucy!

LUCY: Barry, my mother is from Akron and she wants to know if you went to high school with her—

BARRY *(x):* Larry!

LARRY: Why do people insist on calling homosexuals normal? I—

BARRY *(x):* Ralph.

RALPH: I'm in my house. I'm at home, which is where you should be. I'm not far away. Come over if you want. I have some cold cuts. Beer. Come over and we can talk some more. 'Cause you and me, we're the same kind of people. I know you know what I'm talking about. I have beer. Soup. I'm here. Come by later. I'll wait.

(Barry hangs up. He doesn't speak. He takes no calls. Silence.)

SPIKE *(Into in-studio mike):* Barry, forty-five seconds left in the show. *(Beat)* This is dead air, Barry. Dead air.

(Barry closes his eyes. Waits. Forty-five-second pause. Barry opens his eyes, smiles, speaks softly into the on-air mike:)

BARRY: I guess we're stuck with each other. This is Barry Champlain.

(Theme music comes up. Barry stands.)

Monday, Spike.

SPIKE: Monday, Bar.

(Barry leaves the station.

The next host, Susan Fleming, and her operator, Rachael, come in, just as Barry did at the top of his show. Susan Fleming prepares to go on air. She gets her cue and begins her show:)

SUSAN: This is Doctor Susan Fleming. Before I take my first caller, I'd like to comment on something I saw on my way over to the station this evening. There was a man, standing on a street corner, obviously mentally disturbed. It made me think about something we don't often talk about . . .

(Blackout.)

END OF PLAY

On the New York stage, **ERIC BOGOSIAN** has attained singular achieve-ment. In his more than twenty-five-year career, Bogosian has authored five full-length plays and created six full-length solos for himself. For these, he has received three OBIE awards, a Drama Desk Award and an Outer Critics Circle Award. His two best-known plays, *Talk Radio* (The Public Theater/New York Shakespeare Festival) and *subUrbia* (New York's Lincoln Center Theater), have been adapted to film. *Talk Radio*, directed by Oliver Stone, garnered Bogosian the Berlin Film Festival Silver Bear Award for his work as screenwriter and star. Richard Linklater directed the acclaimed film version of *subUrbia*. Bogosian's credits as playwright also include *Griller* (Chicago's Goodman Theatre), *Humpty Dumpty* (Princeton's McCarter Theatre Center), *Red Angel* (Williamstown Theatre Festival) and *Bitter Sauce* (New York's The Acting Company). His solos include *Sex, Drugs, Rock & Roll*; *Pounding Nails in the Floor with My Forehead* and *Drinking in America*. He has toured throughout the United States and Europe, and his solos and plays have been per-formed by acting companies internationally. In 2004 he was awarded a Guggenheim Fellowship to continue his work in the theater.

Bogosian has made numerous appearances as a film and tele-vision actor, working with leading directors, such as Robert Altman, Paul Schrader, Woody Allen, Taylor Hackford and Atom Egoyan. He has starred in a great variety of films, from *Dolores Claiborne* to *Under Siege II*. He recently played Satan in Stephen Adly-Guirgis's play *The Last Days of Judas Iscariot* at The Public Theater. Currently, he stars on *Law & Order: Criminal Intent*.

In June 2005 Bogosian published his second novel, *Wasted Beauty*. Earlier prose includes *Mall* and *Notes from Underground*.

Bogosian lives in New York with his wife, director Jo Bonney, and their two children.

To read more: www.ericbogosian.com